INTERACTIVE METHOD OF TEACHING SCIENCE

LESSON PLANS FOR PRIMARY SCHOOL

DR. RENI FRANCIS

ISBN 979-888591566-3

"To all our teachers for their relentless efforts in fostering science in the classroom"

Contents

Acknowledgements   *vii*

1. Science Learning   1

2. Lesson Plans In Science - 1   4

3. Lesson Plans In Science - 2   8

4. Lesson Plans In Science - 3   12

5. Lesson Plans In Science - 4   16

6. Lesson Plans In Science - 5   22

7. Lesson Plans In Science - 6   27

8. Lesson Plans In Science - 7   33

9. Lesson Plans In Science - 8   42

10. Lesson Plans In Science - 9   50

11. Lesson Plans In Science - 10   57

12. Lesson Plans In Science - 11   60

13. Lesson Plans In Science - 12   64

14. Lesson Plans In Science - 13   71

15. Lesson Plans In Science - 14   78

16. Conclusion   82

17. References   86

Disclaimer   87

Acknowledgements

"Every good and perfect gift is from above, coming down from the Father of the heavenly lights, who does not change like shifting shadows."

James 1:17

At the outset let me thank Almighty God for giving me an opportunity to pen down my thoughts towards this book.

Thanking my family for their continuous support always thus helping to tread through newer path each day.

Thanking my teachers and mentors for their kind motivation.

This book is a humble effort in putting few Science lesson plan that can be implemented in classroom thus celebrating National Science Day on 28th February, 2022.

Science Learning

Science is the systematic study of the structure and behavior of the physical, social, and natural worlds through observation and experimentation. It's key to innovation, global competitiveness, and human advancement. It's important that the world continues to advance the field of science, whether it's finding new cures for cancer and other diseases or identifying and exploring new galaxies.

The Value of Learning Science

Beyond the potential scientific breakthroughs, there are individual benefits to learning science, such as developing our ability to ask questions, collect information, organize and test our ideas, solve problems, and apply what we learn. Even more, science offers a powerful platform for building confidence, developing communication skills, and making sense of the world around us—a world that is increasingly shaped by science and technology.

Science also involves a lot of communication with other people and develops patience and perseverance in children. Finding answers to their countless "why" questions pushes children to research and form their own opinions instead of taking others' for granted. While it's easy to go along with another child's answer or pull out a smartphone and do a quick internet search to know why the leaves fall from the trees, a healthy dose of skepticism can take children farther as they explore the world around them and tackle some of its challenging questions.

Importance of Science learning:

- **Skill Sets:** Science teaches children necessary skills that they can use in other areas of their lives. Kidsource.com reports, "Early experiences in science help children develop problem-solving skills and motivate them toward a lifelong interest in the natural world."

- **Future Resources:** Students who study science early on are better equipped to handle scientific issues facing our world in the future. Prominent issues facing us include land use and development, availability of energy and mineral resources, water resources and quality, preservation of wetlands, erosion, waste management, pollution remediation and geological hazards. Students who are familiar with these issues through science classes may be able to solve some of these problems as adults.

- **Foundations of Learning:** If we want high school students to study science, we need to start by teaching them when they are in elementary school. We cannot expect a high school student to understand the complexities of biology and chemistry if they were never given a foundation of science education at a younger age.

- **Future Careers:**Many important careers require a knowledge of science. Students who want careers in areas such as medicine, environmental work or engineering need a strong foundation in science education in order to obtain those careers.

- **Creative Exploration**: Young minds are creative, innovative and full of ideas. Science nurtures these aspects of the brain. Science dominates our lives and presents society with tremendous opportunities and tremendous challenges." If we want our students to take those opportunities and meet those challenges, we must teach them science at the elementary level and continue to do so at the secondary level.

CHAPTER TWO

Lesson Plans in Science - 1

Producers and Consumers

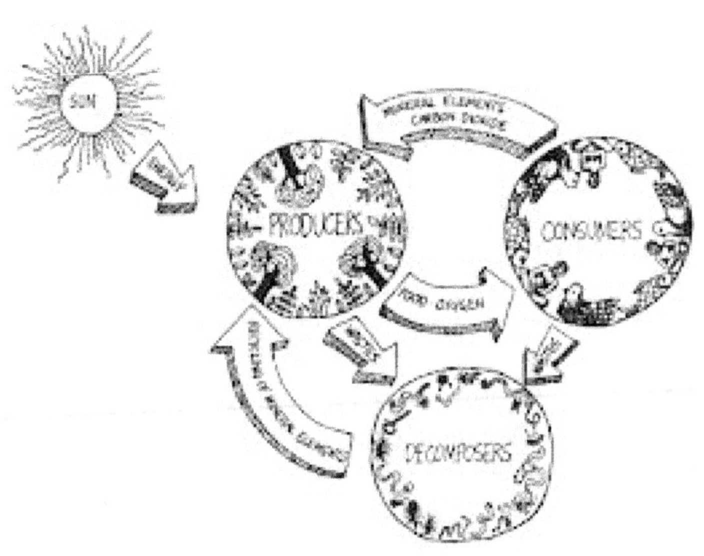

Producers and Consumers

Learning Objectives

Students will be able to differentiate between producers and consumers.

Introduction

Tell your students that today they will be learning about producers and consumers. Ask your students if they know what a producer and consumer are.

Teacher activity

Explain to your students that a **producer** is a creature that makes its own food. An example of a producer is a plant.

Explain to your students that a **consumer** is a creature who eats food made by someone else.

Explain to your students that there are two types of consumers. First level consumers are herbivores who eat plants. Second level consumers are carnivores. Carnivores eat herbivores.

Ideate

Ask your students to get into groups of three.

Ask each group to write a script that has a producer, a first level consumer, and a second level consumer. The script should express the feelings of each character.

Ask each student to draw a mask for their character using paper plates. After that, have each group come up and act out their skit.

An example could be the plant being a producer, a rabbit being a first level consumer, and a lion being a second level consumer.

Design

Ask each student to write a paragraph explaining the role of a producer, a first level consumer, and a second level consumer.

Ask your students to write why each one is important to the ecosystem

Engage: Ask your students to get a shoe box and cover it using green and brown construction papers. Ask your students to draw a producer, a first level consumer, and a second level consumer on Styrofoam. Ask your students to cut it out and cover it with the appropriate color of the animal using construction paper. Ask your students to stick them in the shoe box. Tell your students that they have to connect. An example of connecting could be that a lion eats the rabbit while the rabbit eats the grass.

Tell them to draw pictures of trees, leaves and their first and second level consumers on the sides of the box as well. They could also draw and color on white paper to cut and stick on the box.

Elaborate Ask your students to draw three bubble organizers. Each top bubble should have 3-5 smaller bubbles attached. Ask your students to label the top bubbles producers, first level consumers, and second level consumers. Ask your students to fill the bottom bubbles with their respective examples.

Experiment

Say six plants or animals out loud.

Ask your students to identify them as a producer, a first level consumer, or a second level consumer on notebook paper.

Assessment

Ask your students to get in a circle.

Name an animal and ask the first student to identify it as a producer, a first level consumer, or a second level consumer. Ask that student to say another animal or plant. Have the next student identify the plant or animal that the first student said and say another animal or plant.

Go around the circle until all students get a turn.

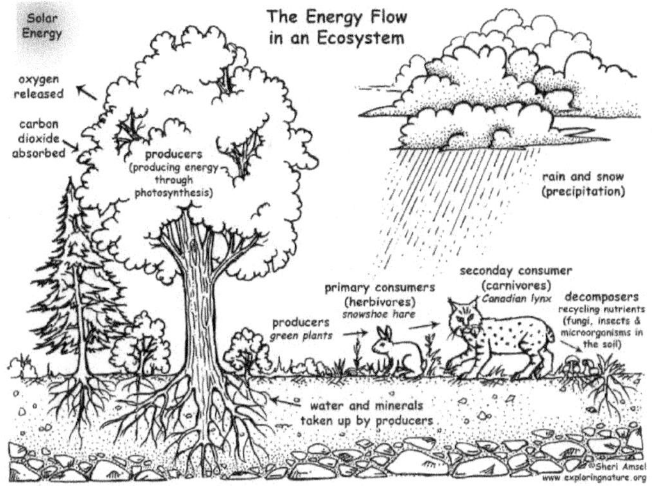

Ecosystem

CHAPTER THREE

Lesson Plans in Science - 2

States of Matter

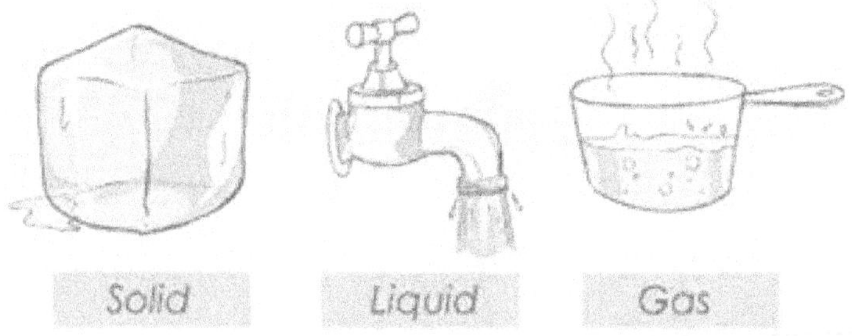

States of Matter

Learning Objectives

Students will be able to describe each state of matter in terms of its molecular structure.

Introduction

Tell students that they are going to learn about solids, liquids, and gases, or **states of matter.**

Ask students if they know what a **molecule** is.

Explain that a molecule is the smallest amount of something and that molecules are so small that they can't even be seen with eyes! Tell your students that everything is made up of molecules.

Tell students that the way molecules move within an object or substance determines whether it is a solid, liquid, or gas.

Teacher activity

Hand out lined paper to each student for note-taking. Draw a square on the whiteboard and label it *solid.*

Fill the square with tiny circles that touch each other. Tell students that these circles represent molecules.

Explain that the molecules in a **solid** are packed tightly together and move slightly in place. Underneath the square, write that solids have a definite shape and definite volume. Have students copy this in their notes.

Draw another square on the board and label it *liquid.* Draw circles that are still somewhat close together but do not fill the entire square and are not in perfectly straight rows.

Explain that the molecules in a **liquid** are close together and can touch each other, but they can also flow and move around.

Underneath this square, write that liquids do not have a definite shape but have a definite volume. Have students copy this in their notes.

Draw a third square on the board. Draw circles that are spaced apart, with lines or arrows around them to show quick movement. Draw a few circles outside of the box.

Explain that molecules in a **gas** move around freely and quickly. They can bump into and bounce off of each other and do not stay in a container unless the container has a lid on it.

Underneath this square, write that gases do not have a definite shape or volume.

Ideate

Explain that students will be demonstrating the molecules in each state of matter.

Start with solids. Have students stand shoulder to shoulder with each other and move slightly back and forth while staying in place.

Next, have students demonstrate the molecules in a liquid. Students should be walking around the room but staying close to their classmates, carefully brushing into one another as they walk around.

Then, have students demonstrate gas. Have students walk quickly (or run, depending on the nature of the space being used). As they carefully make contact with other students, they should walk or run in another direction. Have them spread around the entire space.

Design

Explain to your students that they will be making a substance using cornstarch and water called "goop." Show students how to put the cornstarch in the mixing bowl and slowly add the water. You can also add two drops of food coloring if desired.

Tell students that after making the goop, they will have several minutes to play with it!

Lay down newspapers at students' work stations and pass out the materials to students. Designate tasks for each student. For example, designate someone to pour the water, someone to stir, etc.

Write the following questions on the board for students to discuss within their groups: *What do you think the molecules in goop look like, and why? What state of matter do you think goop is, and why?*

Give students time to clean up.

Enrichment: Have students research other states of matter (colloids and plasma) and share their findings with the class.

Support: Have students use their notes as they answer the discussion questions.

Experiment

Hand out an index card to each student.

Have students describe the molecules in each state of matter without using their notes.

Assessment

Ask students to share their responses to the discussion questions with the class. Call on several volunteers.

Explain that goop is a **colloid,** which is like an "in-between" state of matter because it has properties of a solid and a liquid.

Give students some other real-life examples of colloids, such as butter, shaving cream, lotion, and ketchup.

Ask if students can think of any other colloids.

Challenge students to create a list of solids, liquids, gases, and colloids that they see around their homes!

CHAPTER FOUR

Lesson Plans in Science - 3

Types of Forests

Learning Objectives

Students will be able to identify and describe the four types of forests.

Reading matter:

Types of Forests

Introduction

Tell your students that they will be learning about the four different types of forests today. Write the names of the forests on the board, using the handout as a guide.

Teacher activity:

Go over the Types of Forests handout.

Ideate

Ask your students to get into groups of four. Give each group a white cardboard box.

Ask your students to draw each forest on the four sides by using the Types Of Forests handout. Ask your students to put the title and names of all group members on top.

Design

Ask your students to complete the Four Types Of Forests worksheet.

Enrichment: Ask your students to write an explanation in paragraph format for each side of the box they created in guided practice. Ask your students to write at least two questions about each side. Ask your students to present the box to the support students by pointing to pictures on the sides as well as by reading the paragraph they wrote out loud. After that, ask your students to ask the questions they wrote to the support students.

Support: Listen to the presentations created by enrichment students. Answer the questions that the enrichment students ask verbally and on paper.

Experiment

Grade the worksheet that your students completed to check for understanding.

Assessment

Ask your students to describe the type of forest they would want to live in and why.

Go around the class to give each student an opportunity to answer the question verbally.

Types of Forests

DECIDUOUS

They have warm, wet summers and cold winters. They have Maple and Oak trees. The large flat leaves that drop down each fall grow back each spring. The trees that lose and regrow leaves are called deciduous. They change colors when leaves drop. The species found in these forests include shrubs, mosses, ferns, insects, spiders, snakes, frogs, birds, rabbits, deer, and bears.

TROPICAL RAIN

They are found in Hawaii and Costa Rica. They are hot and wet all year. The leaves stay green all year. There are more living things that live here compared to any other forest. The animals and plants live from top to ground. The species include lizards, rodents, and frogs.

COASTAL

It is thick with tall trees. It is not too warm or cold. There is a lot of rain. The species include flying fox and Pemba, Green pigeon.

CONIFEROUS

They have very cold winters and cool summers. Conifers have seeds in cones and needle-like leaves. A few examples include pines and spruces. They stay green all year which is why they are called Evergreen. They get less rain comparatively but the sharp needles prevent them from losing water. They are shaped like triangles which prevents snow from piling up on branches. They have lakes and streams. The species include squirrels, moose, wolves, insects, and flies.

Four types of Forests

1. Type of Forest
2. Species Found

3. Temperature
4. Trees and Plants Found

CHAPTER FIVE

Lesson Plans in Science - 4

The Solar System

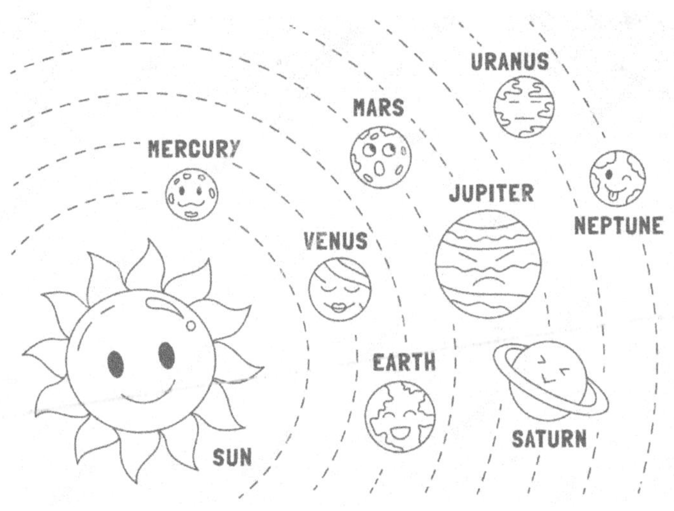

Solar System

Learning Objectives

Students will be able to identify the planets in the Earth's solar system. Students will be able to determine the position of the planets from the sun.

Introduction

Tell your students that they will be learning about the planets today. Ask your students if they can name the planets.

List the names of the planets on the board.

Teacher activity

Ask your students if they know where each planet is located in relation to the Earth.

Explain to your students that there is a trick to remembering the planets in relation to the sun. Explain to your students that they can easily remember the planets' relation to the sun if they memorize the sentence, *My Very Energetic Mother Just Served Us Nachos.*

Explain that the first letter of each word in that acronym represents the name of a planet in relation to the sun.

Ideate

Ask your students to complete the worksheet Our Solar System with a partner. Remind them to use the acronym to help them complete the worksheet.

Design

Give each student the Planet Crossword Puzzle worksheet.

Complete the crossword as a class by asking students to guess which planet is represented by each picture. Tell students a fact or two about each planet as you have them fill out the crossword. For example, Saturn has rings, Pluto used to be considered a full planet, and Jupiter has a famous red spot.

Take your students to the library.

Look out for a few books on planets for the students. Direct each student to pick a planet.

Ask the students to take their Research a Planet worksheets to the library. Have them fill out the worksheet as they look through books about their planets in the library.

Ask students to finish their research at home if they don't finish by checking out books related to their planets.

Instruct students to write a few more facts about their planets on notebook paper.

Enrichment: Instruct your students to complete the Make a Planet worksheet. This activity will make students think creatively about what they would like to have in a planet.

Support: Ask students to draw and color a picture of the solar system. This will enable students to visualize the position of the planets in relation to the sun. Have them label the names of the planets using the *My Very Energetic Mother Just Served Us Nachos* acronym.

Experiment

Ask students to take out a sheet of paper and answer questions about the planets. Potential questions include: *Which planet is closest to the sun? Which planet is the farthest from the sun? Which planets are closest to the Earth? Which is the fourth planet in the solar system?*

Assessment

Ask students to present their Research a Planet worksheet to the class along with other facts that they found.

Name   **Date**

MAKE A PLANET

Billions and billions of stars thrive in our universe, and many more planets orbit around those very stars. Astronomers and space enthusiasts hope that one day we will find a planet like Earth and work towards inhabiting it.

Scientists have just discovered a new planet. Draw a picture of it and come up with ways that humans can live on this planet in harmony with its environment.

What is the name of your planet?________________________________

How will people be able to live there?________________________________

What steps will you take to protect the planet's environement? ________

____

____

Name the planet

Fill up

Across

Crossword

Lesson Plans in Science - 5

Recycling

Recycling

Learning Objectives

Students will be able to determine solutions for encouraging recycling in their community.

Reading matter

What's Recyclable? (PDF) Recycle Worksheet (PDF)

Introduction

Ask students what they know about recycling.

Teacher activity

Talk about different ways people can recycle.

Ask students what they recycle at home and at school.

Explain that objects can go into three categories when you need to get rid of them: trash, **compost**, objects that can be broken down and used in the soil, and **recycling**, which is generally glass, plastic, and paper that can be broken down and made into new items.

Ideate

Pass out the What is Recyclable? worksheet. Read through the worksheet together as a class. Allow students to color the worksheet.

Have student cut out the "stickers" on the worksheet and glue them on the correct objects.

Have a class discussion on ways to help people become aware of recycling and how to recycle appropriately. These ideas may include educating people, putting up posters, coming up with incentives, and making recycling more convenient.

Design

Pass out the Recycle Match-Up worksheet and allow students to complete it. Have students partner up and make an awareness poster about recycling.

When students are done with their posters, encourage them to hang them up around the school or intheir community.

Enrichment: Students may make more than one poster, using a different idea for each poster created.

Support: Students may need guidance in what direction to create their poster. Give these students two options to choose from to use on their poster, such as recycling helps save the earth, or recycling paper in the classroom.

Experiment

Students will be assessed by the completion of their worksheets and the effort put into the posters they've created.

Assessment

Have students share their posters with the rest of the class.

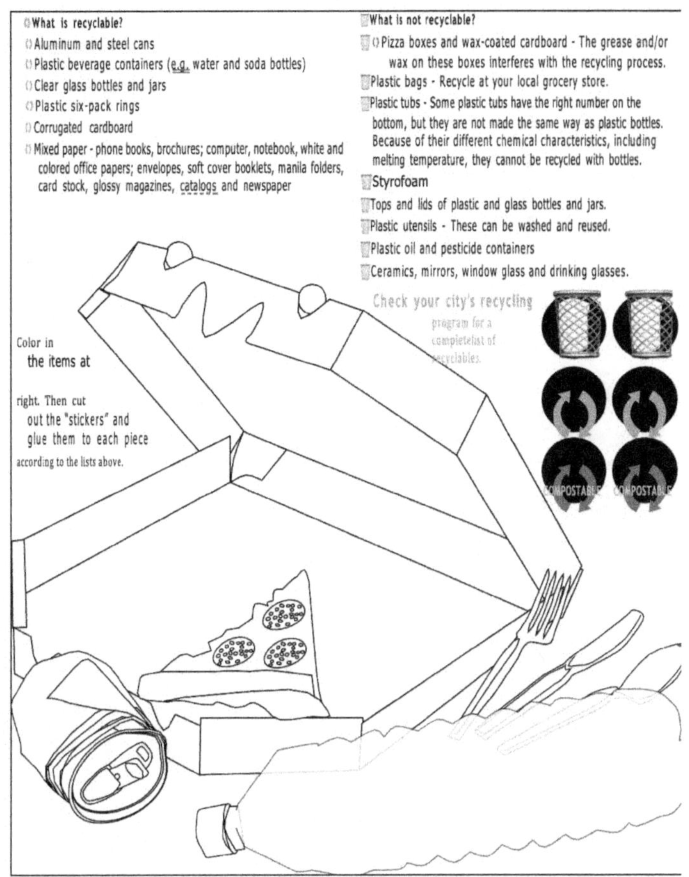

Recycling matter

Recycle
Match-Up

Color each item and draw a line to match it to the correct bin!

(Hint: Aluminum items are usually silver, shiny, and can be crushed.)

PAPER

PLASTIC
&
GLASS

ALUMINUM

Choose the correct basket

CHAPTER SEVEN

Lesson Plans in Science - 6

Vertebrates and Invertebrates

Learning Objectives

Students will be able to identify and define a vertebrate and an invertebrate. Students will be able to classify animals as a vertebrate or an invertebrate.

Reading matter

- Animal Classes (PDF)
- Identify Invertebrates and Vertebrates (PDF)

Introduction

Tell your students that they will be learning about **vertebrates** and **invertebrates**. Tell your students that a vertebrate has a backbone while an invertebrate does not. Ask your students if they are vertebrates or invertebrates.

Teacher activity

Tell your students to draw two columns and label them *vertebrates* and *invertebrates*. Tell them to write the different types for each kind in their columns as you explain them.

Tell your students that there are five main types of vertebrates: mammals, reptiles, fish, birds, and amphibians. Write these on the board.

Give your students examples of each type, such as humans, crocodiles, goldfish, parrots, and frogs. Tell your students that there are five main types of invertebrates: protozoa, echinoderms, annelids, mollusks, and arthropods. Write these on the board and ask your students to write them in the second column.

Offer examples of each, such as algae and bacteria, starfish, earthworms, octopi, and spiders. Tell your students to write the example that you give next to each kind in their columns as well.

Ideate

Ask your students to complete the Identify Invertebrates and Vertebrates worksheet with a partner. Go over the worksheet as a class.

Design

Have your students complete the Animal Classes worksheet. Go over the worksheet as a class.

Enrichment: Ask your students to pick an invertebrate. Have them go to the library and find a book on that invertebrate. Ask your students to find and write five facts about that particular invertebrate. Tell them to draw a picture of the invertebrate as well.

Support: Have your students come to the back of the class. Give them each ten index cards. Tell them to write the five kinds of vertebrates on five of the cards. They should use one card per kind. Show them a picture of each kind on the computer. Ask them to draw the picture on their card. Repeat this for invertebrates.

Experiment

Conduct a short quiz on vertebrates and invertebrates. Potential questions include: *Which type of animal has a backbone? Which type of animal does not have a backbone? Name any two types of vertebrates. Name any two types of invertebrates.*

Assessment

Ask your students to pick a vertebrate and an invertebrate.

Instruct them to draw them on white paper. Ask your students to write the name of the vertebrate and invertebrate as well.

Animal Classes

Scientists have organized animals into different groups in order to make them easier to study. It's time for you to put on your scientist hat and match the following animals to the class that they belong to.

Vertebrates are animals with a backbone. Can you guess what an invertebrate is?

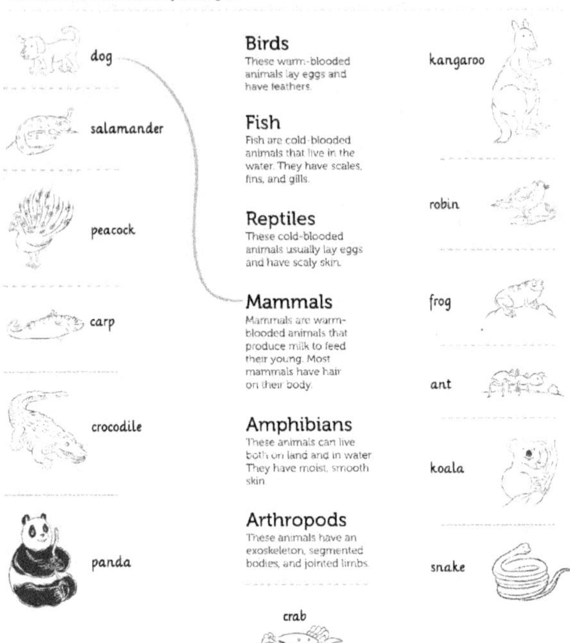

Vertebrates and Invertebrates

Name ___________________________ **Date** ___________________________

IDENTIFY INVERTEBRATES AND VERTEBRATES

Many different animals share our planet with us. Many are alike, and many are different. Scientists **classify** animals based on their similarities. One way scientists group animals is whether or not those animals have a backbone.

Some animals, like dogs, cats, birds, lizards, fish, and even humans have backbones - Scientists classify backboned animals as **vertebrate**.

Other animals, such as squid, worms, bugs, and clams do not have backbones. Scientists call these animals **invertebrates.**

Choose **five animals** from the list below. Write the animal's name, whether
it is a vertebrate or invertebrate, and two important traits in the
spreadsheet.An example has been provided for you.

Scorpion **Fox** **Octopus** **Snail** ~~**Rabbit**~~ **Wolf** **Deer**

T-Rex **Spider** **Fish** **Jellyfish** **Turtle** **Beetle** **Hawk**

Animal	Vertebrate / Invertebrate	Two important traits
Rabbit	Verteb rate	1. A rabbit has long ears. 2. A rabbit is a mammal.

CHAPTER EIGHT

Lesson Plans in Science - 7

States Of Matter: Identifying Solids, Liquids, and Gases

The States of Matter

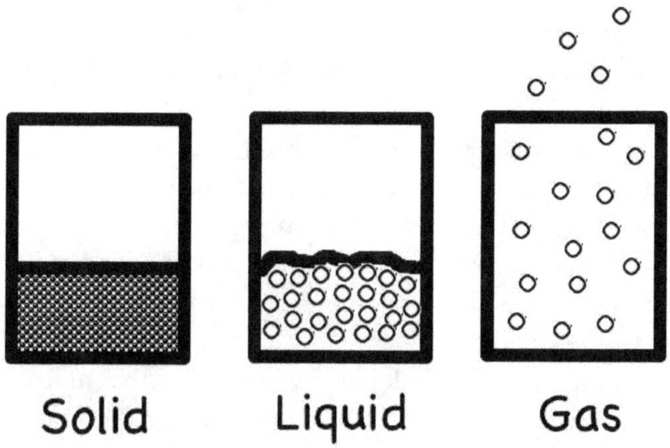

States of Matter

Learning Objectives

Students will be able to differentiate between a solid, liquid, and gas. Students will be able to give examples of changes in states of matter from heating and cooling.

Reading matter

Drawing Solids, Liquids, and Gases (PDF) Solid, Liquid, Gas (PDF)

What is Gas? (PDF) What is Liquid? (PDF) What is Solid? (PDF)

Matter Mixup: What's a Solid? (PDF) Matter Mixup: What's a Liquid? (PDF) Matter Mixup: What's a Gas? (PDF)

Matter Mixup: Drawing Solids, Liquids, and Gases (PDF) Matter Mixup: What's a Solid? (PDF)

Matter Mixup: What's a Liquid? (PDF) Matter Mixup: What's a Gas? (PDF)

Matter Mixup: Drawing Solids, Liquids, and Gases (PDF)

Introduction

Tell your students that they will be learning about the states of matter.

Explain that everything in our lives is made up of matter. It includes the air we breathe, the clothes we wear, the books we read, the food we eat, etc.

Ask them if they know what the 3 states of matter are. List the three states of matter on the board.

Teacher activity

Define the word **molecule** by explaining that molecules are what is in all matter. Molecules are the smallest possible amount of a substance.

Explain to your students that a **solid** is something that keeps its own shape because the molecules are packed tightly together. Have your students come up with examples, and write them on the board. Offer examples, such as desks, books, and chairs.

Remind your students that a **liquid** is something that doesn't have its own shape because the molecules are more loosely packed together. Liquids take the shape of whatever container they are put in. Some examples include water and juice. Ask your students to come up with additional examples of liquids. List them on the board.

Explain to your students that a **gas** has no particular shape because the molecules are spaced apart and move around freely. They move around and can fit any container they're put in. Tell your students that air is made of gases, and share that gas usually can't be seen.

Pose the following question: Can a solid turn into a liquid? Give students time to think, pair with a partner to discuss, and then share with the whole group.

Explain that a cube of ice can turn into a liquid with heat. Place a cube of ice in warm water, and have your students observe it for 5 minutes. Show your students how the ice is starting to melt.

Ask your students if a liquid can turn into a gas. Have them think, pair with a partner to discuss, and share with the whole group. Then, demonstrate the change in the state of matter by placing a glass of water in a microwave. Set the microwave to 3 minutes. Take out the cup and show students that the bubbles formed on top of the water consist of gas.

Design

Ask your students to complete the Solid, Liquid, Gas worksheet with a partner. Go over the worksheet as a class.

Experiment

Ask your students to complete the What is Solid?, What is Liquid?, and What is Gas? worksheets. Go over these worksheets with your students.

Enrichment: Instruct your students to research what would happen to their body without liquids. Have them come up with two facts in their own words. Direct your students to find out the different gases that make up the air and their roles. Ask your students to research and explain 2 things that would happen to the Earth if it weren't solid.

Support: Instruct your students to complete the Drawing Solids, Liquids, and Gases worksheet. Help them come up with examples for each state. This worksheet will give students a visual about the three different categories.

Ask your students to give an example of a time when a solid can change into a liquid. Have them explain when a liquid can change into a gas.

Instruct them to write down the answers on a sheet of paper.

Assessment

Go around the class, and ask your students to give an example of a solid and a liquid.

Tell your students that for a gas, they can describe a process that consists of releasing gas such as breathing or burping. Alternatively, give an example of a gas found in the air such as oxygen or nitrogen.

Write examples of solid, liquid, gases

Draw a line connecting the pictures on the left to the matching phase of matter on the right.

Do it yourself...

Do it yourself...

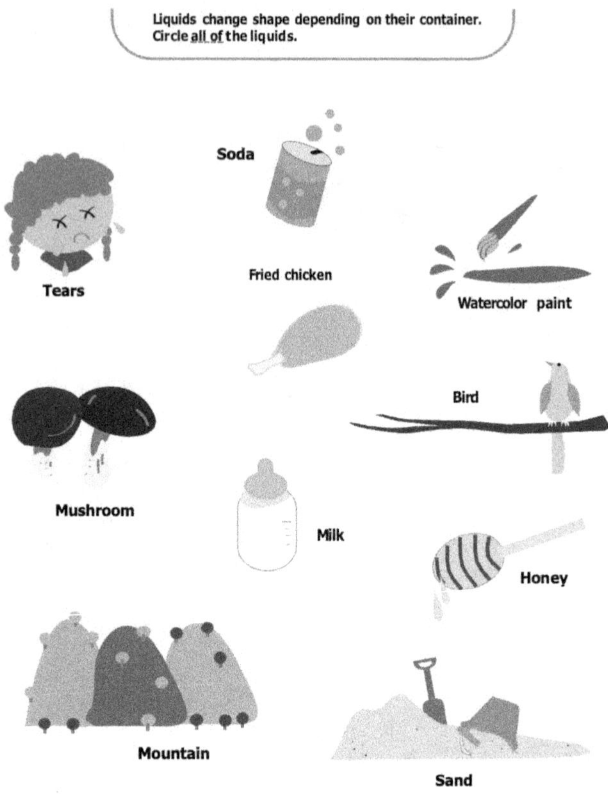

Do it yourself...

Do it yourself...

CHAPTER NINE

Lesson Plans in Science - 8

Natural Resources

Natural Resources

Learning Objectives

Students will be able to define a natural resource. Students will be able to identify the main natural resources present in the Earth.

Reading Matter:

- Plant Resources (PDF)
- Soil Resources (PDF)
- Water Resources (PDF)
- Natural Resources Word Find (PDF)

Introduction

To begin the lesson, ask your students to tell you the first thing they think of when they hear each of these words: plant, water, soil.

Ask your class is anyone knows what a natural resource is. Encourage your students to make educated guesses.

Once the class has come up with a few answers, explain that a **natural resource** is a substance found in the Earth naturally.

Teacher Activity

Write the words plants, soil, and water on the board. Explain that these are the three main types of natural resources.

Start a class discussion about the importance of plants. Great questions include: *Why are plants important? Could we live without plants? How do plants help us stay alive? How do plants help animals?* Explain that plants provide us with food, oxygen to help us breathe, and protection through homes and fire. Plants make and protect soil, feed animals, shelter animals, and are used to make clothes and many medicines.

Ask your students about the importance of soil. Great discussion questions include: *What is soil? Why is it important? What would our lives be like without soil? Could we live without it? Why or why not?*

Share that soil contains important nutrients that plants and humans need to stay alive. Soil also helps plants retain the moisture they need to grow and thrive. Finally, ask your students about the importance of water. Suggested questions include: *Could we live without water? What about plants and animals? How long could someone survive without water?*

Explain that water is the most essential natural resource that the Earth gives us, and that plants, animals, and people would die without it.

Ideate

Pair off students a partner, or ask them to find someone to work with.

Assign each pair the Water Resources, Plant Resources, and Soil Resources worksheets to complete together.

Design

Ask your students to complete the Natural Resources Word Find.

Enrichment: Ask your students to pick a topic out of plants, water, and soil to research. Send these students to the library to choose a book about their topic, or assist them with getting online. Each student should write five benefits about their topic that they learned from the book.

Support: Ask your students to draw two columns on a sheet of paper. Ask them to label the first column *Know* and the second column *Learned*. Ask your students to write information they know about plants, soil, and water in the know column. Together, review the information that they know, and discuss some things they may not know. Afterward, instruct them to fill the *Learned* column with the new information that they learned.

Experiment

Ask your students to write one benefit of plants, one benefit of water, and one benefit of soil in their notebooks or on sheets of lined paper.

Assessment

Ask your students to present one of their worksheets from the guided practice to the class.

Encourage your class to find three objects at home that were made, directly or indirectly, using plants, water, and soil.

**Plants are a natural resource that people and <u>animals</u> use.
Below are some examples. Write down more examples and draw a picture of
your favorite one.**

1. Trees provide shelter for animals.

2. ____

3. ____

4. ____

5. ____

6. ____

Do it yourself...

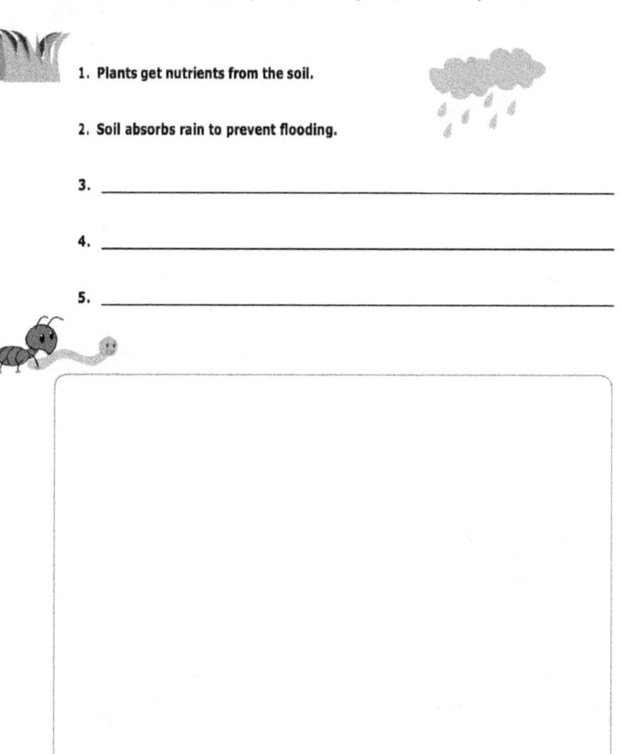

Soil is a natural resource that helps people and animals. Below are some examples. Write down more examples and draw a picture of the one you like best.

1. **Plants get nutrients from the soil.**

2. **Soil absorbs rain to prevent flooding.**

3. _______________________________________

4. _______________________________________

5. _______________________________________

Do it yourself...

Water is a natural resource that people use in everyday life.
Look at the descriptions below and draw pictures to illustrate them.

Agricultural

Farmers use water to grow crops.

Industrial

We build dams for power generation.

Household

We use water for bathing everyday.

Recreation

We go sailing in the lake.

Do it yourself...

NATURAL RESOURCES WORD FIND

Natural resources are nonliving things from nature that are used to support life on Earth. Can you find 8 examples of natural resources in the word find below?

O	E	Q	Y	D	A	U	H	P	W	R
B	J	S	O	I	L	P	W	E	A	P
F	O	S	S	I	L	F	U	E	L	S
U	A	U	D	X	B	F	E	N	C	F
I	N	V	C	F	E	W	A	T	E	R
D	I	A	H	U	W	G	B	R	F	W
E	M	I	N	E	R	A	L	S	R	V
W	A	R	Y	D	L	H	O	U	S	H
X	L	P	U	M	O	R	T	N	A	U
E	S	Q	L	K	P	R	F	L	P	R
Y	I	A	M	A	I	A	T	I	H	E
O	E	X	F	M	N	X	I	G	K	C
E	V	S	D	W	C	T	O	H	L	B
W	T	E	W	O	G	Y	S	T	E	F
R	N	A	I	F	E	C	V	D	O	S

WATER	AIR	SOIL
PLANTS	FOSSIL FUELS	SUNLIGHT

Enter Caption

CHAPTER TEN

Lesson Plans in Science - 9

Parts of a Plant

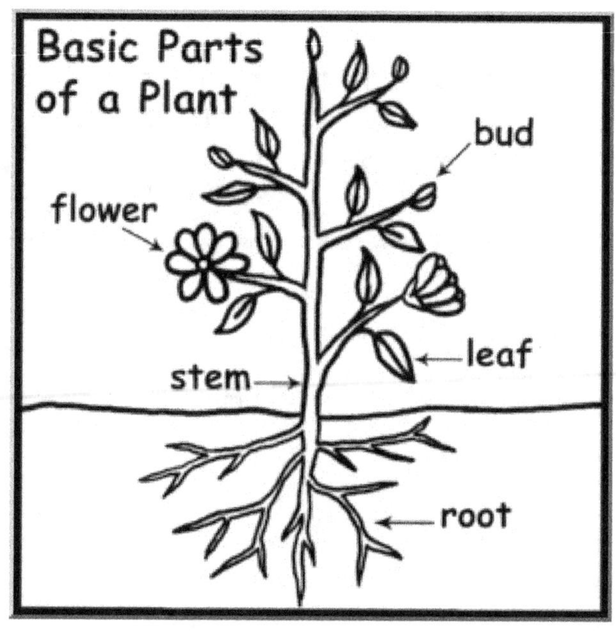

Parts of a Plant

Learning Objectives

Students will be able to identify and describe the basic parts of a plants. Students will be able to describe different kinds of leaves.

Attachments

Leaf Shapes (PDF) Parts of a Plant (Doc)

Life Cycle of a Plant (PDF)

Introduction

Draw a picture of a plant on the board. Be sure to include roots, a stem, a flower, and leaves in your drawing.

Ask your students to tell you what you've just drawn. Once someone answers *plant*, ask your students whether or not anyone can tell you the different parts of a plant.

Allow your students to make suggestions for the labels.

Teacher activity

Once a few students have answered, correctly label the roots, stem, flower, and leaves.

Discuss the parts of the plants with your students. Great potential questions include: *What do the roots do? How do the roots help keep a plant alive? What purpose do leaves serve? What does the stem do?*

What do flowers do?

One by one, explain the function of each plant part.

Tell your class that **roots** hold the plant into the soil. They take in water and minerals to help the plant stay alive.

Define the **stem** as the part that carries water from the roots to the other parts of the plant. Explain that the **flower** helps the plant reproduce, making seeds that will grow into new plants. Tell your class that **leaves** take in the air and light that a plant needs to live.

Display the Leaf Shapes worksheet using an interactive whiteboard, document camera, or projector. Explain that different plants have leaves that are different shapes and sizes.

Give a few examples of plants that have different shapes of leaves. For example, maple trees have star- shaped leaves, magnolia trees have obovate leaves, and birch trees have deltoid leaves.

Use this as a jumping off point for a class discussion about what plants need to survive. After some suggestions, remind your students that plants need sun, water, soil, and air to live.

Ideate

Pass out the following supplies to your class: coffee grounds, fake flowers, green construction paper, glue, scissors, and white construction paper.

Tell your students that they will each be creating a plant that has roots, a stem, leaves, and a flower. Instruct your students to label the parts of their plants using sticky notes. Be sure the Leaf Shapes worksheet is still being displayed, and remind your students to label the type of leaves as well.

Encourage your class to get creative, and invent a name for their plant. They can also invent the uses of their plant.

Design

Ask your students to complete the Parts Of A Plant worksheet independently.

Enrichment: Challenge advanced students to use their new knowledge about the parts of a plant to complete the Life Cycle of a Plant worksheet.

Support: Review the parts of a plant with students who are struggling by removing the labels from their plant. Discuss the roles of each part of a plant, and challenge your student to re-label the plant. Be sure to scaffold the correct labels by discussing the function of each part. That way, every kind of learner will be able to retain this information.

Experiment

Grade the Parts of a Plant worksheets as students finish them.

Assessment

Invite students to present their plants to the class, being sure to share their plants name and function, as well as the parts of their plant and what they're used for.

LEAF CHART

ACTIVITY: LEAF WALK

Go for a walk with an adult and collect 10 leaves with different shapes. Once you're back home, use this chart to figure out what type of leaves you found.

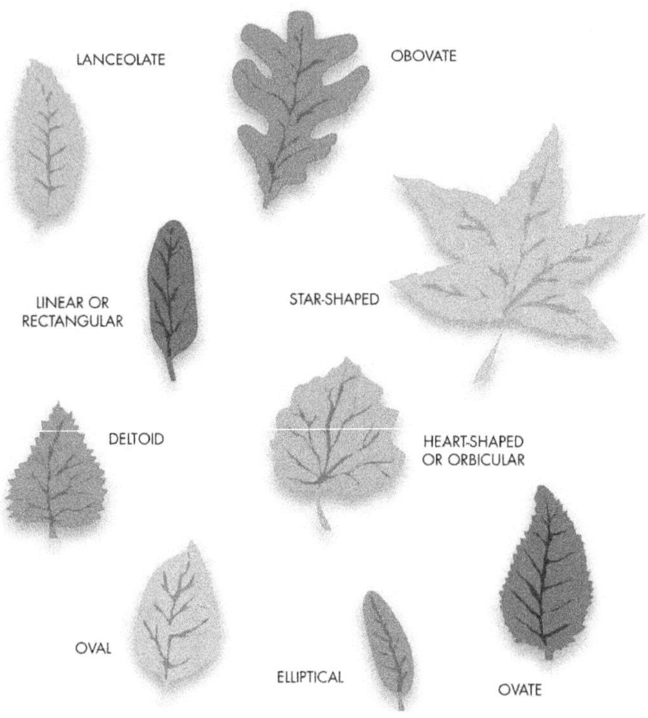

Do it yourself...

Life cycle of a Plant

Plants are living organisms. They use light from the sun to make their own food in the form of a sugar called *glucose*. This process is called *photosynthesis* Plants also get nutrients from the soil through their roots. They breathe in carbon <u>dioxide</u> and they breathe out oxygen.

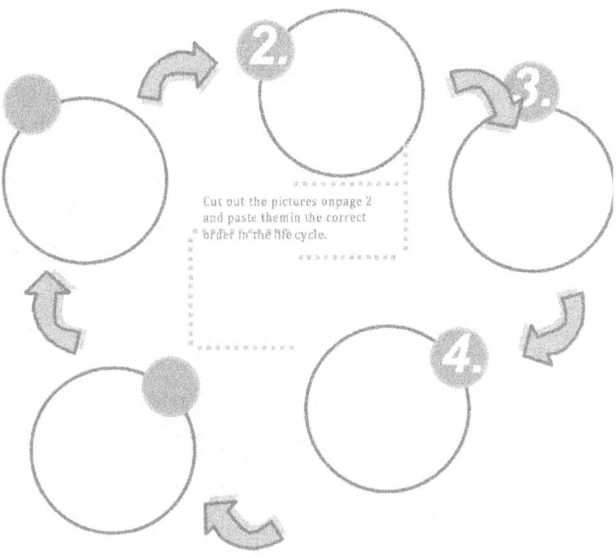

Do it yourself...

Life cycle of a Plant

A plant starts out as a *seed* buried in the ground. As water falls on the seed and the sun warms it, its hard shell opens and it starts to grow out its *roots*. As the plant grows, its *stem* bursts through the soil. Then, *leaves* start to grow out of the stem. As the plant gets bigger it will begin to grow buds, which later sprout into *flowers*, and sometimes those flowers turn into fruit!As bees feed on the nectar, they *pollinate* the plants, allowing more seeds to be m

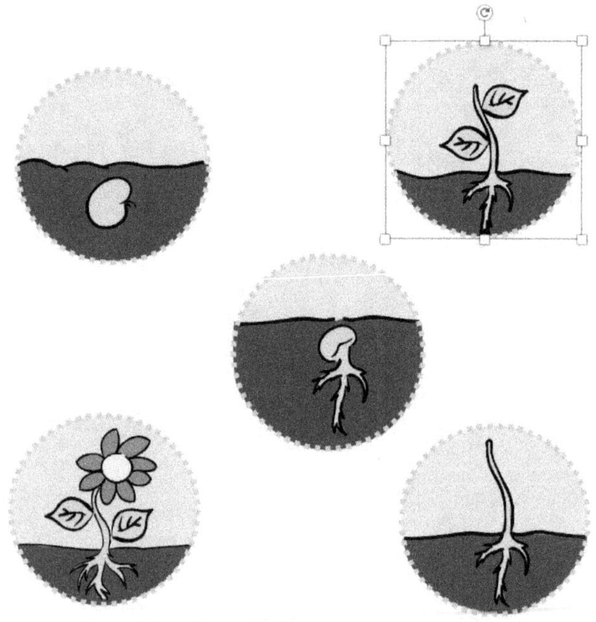

Do it yourself...

CHAPTER ELEVEN

Lesson Plans in Science - 10

Sink or Float

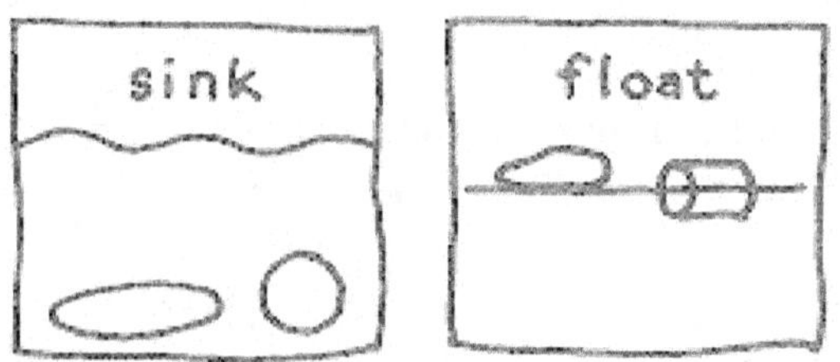

Sink or Float

Learning Objectives

Students will learn the relative densities of different objects.

Reading matter:

Sink or Float (PDF)

Introduction

Ask the students what items they think will sink or float.

Don't make it specific to the items that you are going to use. Let the students give you a list of random items they think will sink or float.

Teacher Activity

Take out the chart with each object listed.

Have the students reflect on whether they think each object with sink or float. Take votes to see who thinks the item will sink and who thinks the item will float. Post the chart to use later for closing the lesson.

Ideate

Pick two of the objects on the Sink or Float worksheet and test out the predictions with the students. Organize students into small teams.

Design

Have students work with their team to finish the rest of the sink or float activity and determine whether their predictions were correct.

Enrichment: Have advanced students journal about other objects that might be on the border for the sink or float discussion.

Support: Give struggling students one-on-one assistance over the course of the lesson.

Experiment

Have you students write down about what they predicted and what the outcome was.

Assessment

Review the predictions. Make changes to the chart if needed.

SINK OR FLOAT

In the spaces below, write if the object will sink or float.

PAPER CLIP

FORK

____

____

SCISSORS

DRINKING STRAW

____

____

FULL BOTTLE OF WATER

BASEBALL

____

____

Do it yourself....

CHAPTER TWELVE

Lesson Plans in Science - 11

All about Rocks

Learning Objectives
Students will be able to define and describe how the three major types of rocks are formed.

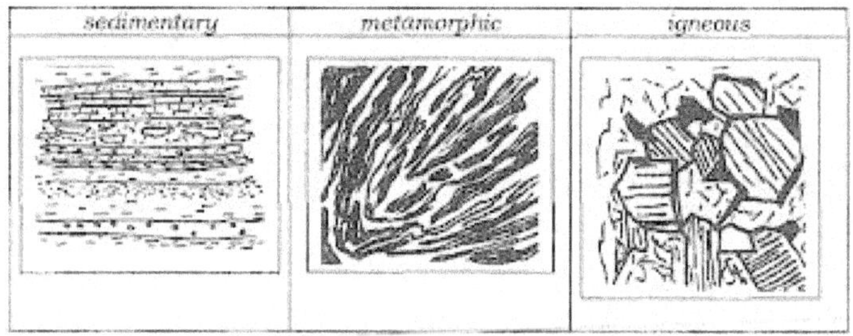

All about Rocks

Introduction
Ask your students what they know about rocks. List their responses on chart paper.

Now ask your students what they want to know about rocks. List their responses on chart paper.

Teacher Activity

Tell your students that there are three different kinds of rocks. The first type is called **igneous**. Igneous rocks are composed of melted rock that hardens and cools. A few examples include obsidian and pumice. Show your students a picture of each example.

Explain that the second type of rock is called **sedimentary**, and they're formed from material that is settled into layers. The layers are squeezed until they harden into rock. A few examples include limestone, breccia, and sandstone. Show your students a picture of each example.

Tell your students that the third type of rock is called **metamorphic**. These rocks are changed by heat and pressure. A few examples include slate and marble. Show your students a picture of each example.

Ideate

Demonstrate each type of rock using the examples below. If the hands-on materials aren't available, simply use each scenario as an analogy to help your students better understand the differences between the three kinds of rocks.

Get an ice tray. Fill it with water and put it in the freezer. After an hour, show your students that an igneous rock is like a cube of ice. It's originally melted, then hardens after being put in the freezer. It's cool when you take it out.

Give your students the example of an omelet for metamorphic rocks. Tell your students that the egg is mixed with various ingredients, and then cooked. The egg experiences heat and pressure from the flames of the stove, which enables it to turn into an omelet.

Display a layered cake to your class, and tell your students that this is similar to how sedimentary rock is formed. Tell them the various layers of the cake come together after baking in the oven.

Design

Place different types of rocks on the table. They could obsidian, pumice, sandstone, or other examples from above.

Ask your students to identify each as igneous, sedimentary, or metamorphic.

Enrichment

Ask your students to complete the All About Me: Rocks Edition worksheet.

Support

Ask your students to create a sandwich using construction paper. Tell them to describe igneous and metamorphic rocks on the slices of bread and sedimentary in the middle.

Experiment

Ask your students to make a graphic poster about either igneous, sedimentary, or metamorphic rocks. On the poster, they should use pictures and words to share how the rocks are formed.

Assessment

Post the graphic posters around the room. Give students time to walk around the room, adding sticky notes with compliments or wonders to each other's posters.

Debrief your class about what everyone noticed about the posters. Return to the "Know" and "Want to Know" charts from the beginning of class. Ask students what they learned about rocks and write their answers on a separate piece of chart paper. Tell students that you can investigate questions that were left unanswered from the "Want to

Know" section on another day.

Rock Cycle

CHAPTER THIRTEEN

Lesson Plans in Science - 12

The Respiratory System

Learning Objectives

Students will be able to identify the parts of the respiratory system. Students will be able to describe the functions of each part of the respiratory system.

Reading matter:

- Are Your Lungs Healthy (PDF)
- Respiratory System (PDF)
- Your Body: Your Lungs (PDF)
- Your Respiratory System (PDF)

Introduction

Tell your students that today they will learn about the respiratory system.

Display a poster and divide it into two columns, with the first column labeled with *know* and the second column labeled with *learned.*

Ask your students what they know about the respiratory system. Write the information in the first column.

Teacher activity

Pass out the Respiratory System worksheet to your students.

Go over the worksheet with your students and explain the function of each part. Ask your students to label the part as you go over it. Instruct your students to write the definition and explanation of each word as you explain it on notebook paper. Explain to your students that the **sinus cavity** is the area around the nose and eyes that cleans the air people breathe in. Inform your students that the **pharynx** is behind the nose and mouth and that the **larynx** is in the neck and contains the vocal cords. Tell them that the **trachea** connects the pharynx and larynx to the lungs and is responsible for the passage of air, while the **bronchi** are small tubes that bring air to and from the lungs.

Remind them that the **lung** is the main part of the respiratory system and puts oxygen into the bloodstream.

Explain that the **diaphragm** is a muscle that moves up and down to expand the lungs. This helps a person breathe.

Ideate

Ask your students to complete the Your Respiratory System worksheet with a partner. Go over the worksheet as a class.

Design

Give each student seven index cards.

Ask your students to write the name of the part on the front of the card. Have them draw the picture of the part on the front of the card as well.

Ask your students to write the description and function of the part on the back of the card.

Enrichment: Ask your students to complete the Are Your Lungs Healthy worksheet. After that, have them research any two different types of lungs from the worksheet. Ask them to write a compare and contrast paragraph on the two different types of lungs.

Support: Ask your students to create two columns on a piece of paper. Have them label the first one *know* and the second one *learn*. Ask them to fill out the *know* column for each part of the respiratory system. Go over the chart and explain the missing parts again. Ask your students to fill out the *learn* column after you finish explaining the parts again.

Experiment

Ask your students to complete the Your Body: Your Lungs worksheet.

Assessment

Ask your students what they learned about the respiratory system, and write it in the second column on the poster board from the introduction.

Are your lungs healthy?

Directions: Compare the healthy pair of lungs to the other types of lungs. How do you think each person's condition affects their ability to breathe?

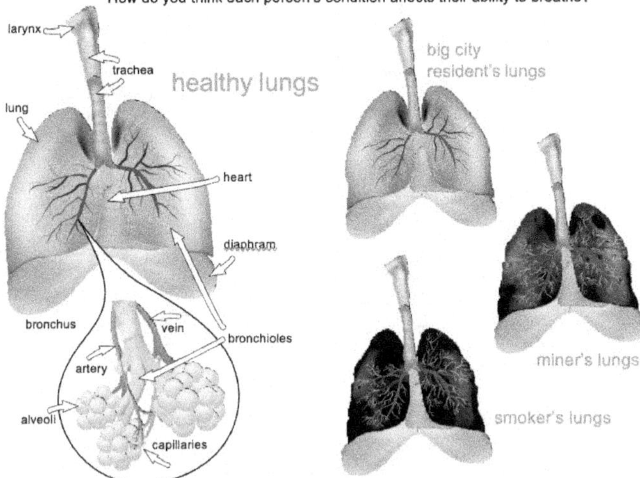

Word Scramble! Use the diagram above to unscramble these names of lung parts.

1. vielaol _______________

2. gnul _______________

3. terary _______________

4. evin _______________

5. tchraae _______________

6. chusbron _______________

7. brchionleo _______________

8. pillapciesa _______________

Do it yourself...

Respiratory System

During inspiration, air passes through the mouth and nose, down the throat, and through the trachea and bronchi to the lungs.

In the lungs, air travels through branching bronchioles which end in small clusters of microscopic sacs called alveoli.

Oxygen molecules are transferred from the alveoli into the bloodstream, and carbon dioxide moves out of the bloodstream and back into the respiratory tract where it is released through the mouth and nose during expiration.

1. sinus cavity
2. pharynx
3. larynx (voice box)
4. trachea (windpipe)
5. bronchi
6. lung
7. diaphragm: *a muscular sheet separating the chest cavity from the abdominal cavity. It contracts to increase room in the chest cavity and draw oxygen into the lungs.*

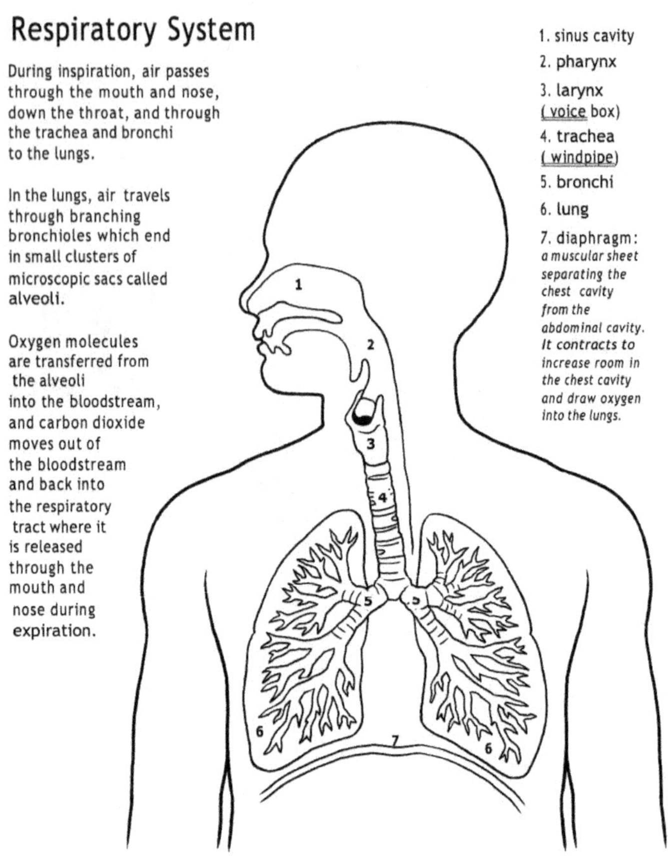

Do it yourself...

YOUR BODY: LUNGS

No other planet in our solar system contains air like ours. The air in our planet contains **oxygen**, which is what humans and animals need to survive. Your **lungs** help take in that oxygen and share it with the rest of your body.

Your body has **two lungs**, and they are the second largest organs in your body (the largest organ is your **skin**). They work together with your **heart** to draw in oxygen, which is carried by **red blood cells** across your body.

A large muscle called the **diaphragm** works with your lungs to get air in and out of your body. It rests just below your lungs, near the upper part of your belly.

When you breathe in (**inhale**), air travels through your **nasal cavity**, where your **nose hairs** filter dust and other gross stuff before it enters your body. Air then travels down the **trachea**, the **pharynx**, and the **larynx** in that order before passing through two large tubes called **bronchi**. These large tubes kind of look like trees, expanding and branching out into the spongy part of your left or right lung.

Your **ribcage** protects this delicate system, and each **rib** embraces a soft, spongy lung on the left or right side of your body so you don't accidentally hurt them.

Use the reading, word bank, and diagram to solve the crossword.

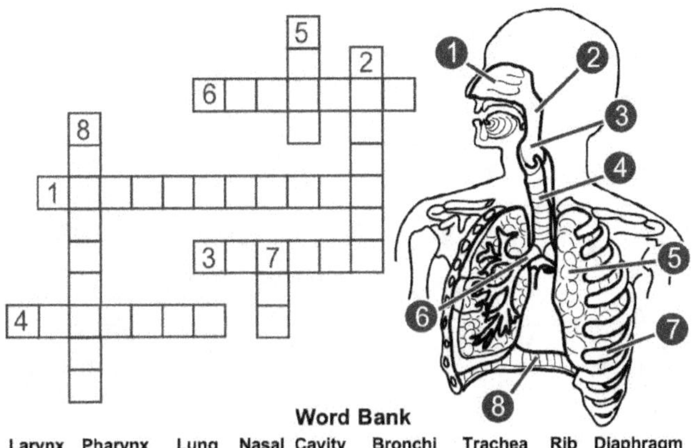

Word Bank

Larynx Pharynx Lung Nasal Cavity Bronchi Trachea Rib Diaphragm

Do it yourself...

Your Respiratory System

Directions: Look at the diagram. Read about what each part of the respiratory system does. Label each part of the respiratory system on the diagram.

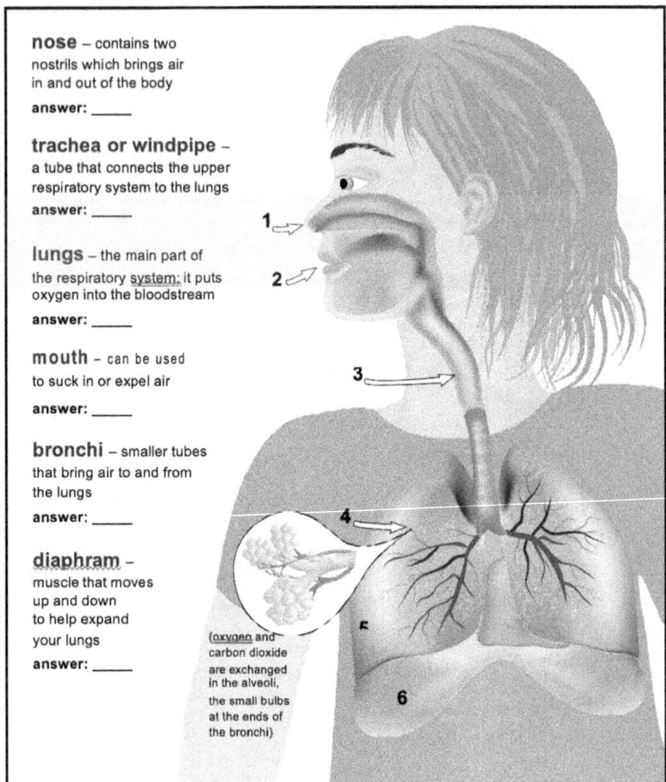

nose – contains two nostrils which brings air in and out of the body

answer: _____

trachea or windpipe – a tube that connects the upper respiratory system to the lungs

answer: _____

lungs – the main part of the respiratory system; it puts oxygen into the bloodstream

answer: _____

mouth – can be used to suck in or expel air

answer: _____

bronchi – smaller tubes that bring air to and from the lungs

answer: _____

diaphram – muscle that moves up and down to help expand your lungs

answer: _____

Enter Caption

CHAPTER FOURTEEN

Lesson Plans in Science - 13

Physical Change and Chemical Change

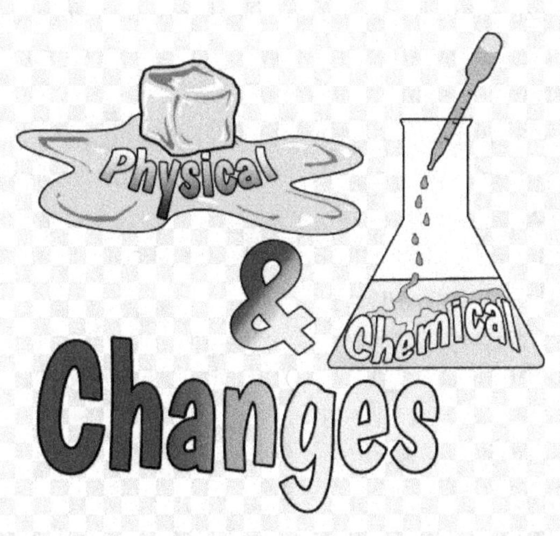

Physical and Chemical Change

Learning Objectives

Students will be able to differentiate between physical and chemical changes. Students will be able to differentiate between physical and chemical properties of matter.

Introduction

Begin the lesson by asking your students what physical and chemical changes they have seen in the environment.

Tell your students that they will be learning about the physical and chemical changes and properties of matter.

Teacher Activity

Pass out the What's the Matter worksheet to your students. Go over the changes and properties with your students.

Explain each change and property to your students with an example.

An example of a physical change would be shape. You can explain that shape is a physical property. For example, a rectangle can be broken down into triangles, but it would still contain the same amount of mass.

Go over and explain the physical and chemical changes to your students on page 2 in the What's the Matter packet.

Ideate

Conduct the experiment on the second page of the What's the Matter packet.

Ask your students to answer the questions about the experiment on the What's the Matter worksheet with a partner.

Go over the questions as a class.

Design

Ask your students to write the definition of each word on page 4 of the packet.

Enrichment

Ask your students to write a paragraph explaining why the metabolism of food is a chemical change. Have them research the metabolism of food before writing the paragraph.

Support

Show your students one example of a physical change and one example of a chemical change through a drawing. An example could be fireworks for a chemical change and cutting a paper for a physical change.

Experiment

Ask your students to complete the Chemical vs. Physical Properties worksheet.

Assessment

Ask your students to pick an object. Have them think of a physical change or chemical change that the object could go through. Instruct your students to write two properties that would change as a result of the change.

Ask your students to share what they wrote with the class.

Reading matter:

What's the Matter?

Matter is anything that takes up space and has mass. **Mass** is the *stuff* that matter is made of, or the amount of particles in a substance or object. Matter has physical and chemical properties and can undergo physical and chemical changes.

What are some examples of matter? Well, just look around you and everything you see, touch, smell, and breathe are examples of matter.

What is a **property**?

A property describes how an object looks, feels, or acts. Properties can be physical or chemical.

Properties can also be quantitative or qualitative. A **qualitative** property of matter is observed and generally can't be measured with a numerical result. A **quantitative** property of matter is one that can be measured numerically, such as height, length, or weight.

What are examples of **physical properties**?

Physical properties can be observed. Examples of physical properties can be color, weight, volume, size, shape, density, boiling point, or freezing point.

What are examples of **chemical properties**?

A chemical property is usually one that can only be seen when a substance undergoes a chemical change. These properties cannot be observed by touching or looking. Chemical properties become apparent when the structure of the substance is altered chemically.

An example of this would be adding baking soda and vinegar and watching it bubble and give off a gas. The bubbling is an indicator that the properties of the two initial ingredients have recombined to form a new substance or substances.

substance AB +substance CD new substance AD + new substance BC A simple equation of what happens when you add baking soda to vinegar:

baking soda (solid) + vinegar (liquid) carbon dioxide (gas) + water (liquid)

What is a **chemical change**?

A **chemical change** is a change that results in a new substance (or substances) being formed. The important word to remember is *new*. A chemical change involves the making or breaking of bonds between atoms. A chemical change makes a new substance that wasn't there before.

What are examples of chemical changes?

Some examples of chemical changes are nails rusting over time, batter turning into a cake in the oven, wood or paper burning to ashes, the digestion of food, and the baking soda and vinegar example above.

What is a **physical change**?

A **physical change** is a change in a state of matter. For example, when ice melts, the H_2O molecule is going from a solid (ice) state to a liquid (water) state of matter. The actual molecule or the arrangement of the atoms has not changed—just its state of matter. A physical change can also be a change in appearance of matter. For example, a piece of paper is made of paper molecules, and when you tear the piece of paper in half, both halves are still made of paper molecules. The atoms and molecules that make up the substance are not physically changed.

<u>Physical or Chemical Change?</u>
Put a check to indicate whether you think the item is a physical change or a chemical change.

	Physical Change	Chemical Change
1. ice melting		
2. cutting a pineapple into pieces		
3. adding vinegar to baking soda		
4. a piece of rusting metal		
5. a campfire		
6. crumbling a piece of paper		
7. sour milk		
8. shattering a drinking glass		
9. dissolving sugar in water		
10. burning paper		
11. boiling water		
12. burning a match		

Do it yourself...

<u>Try This Experiment</u>

How do you know that a gas is produced as a result of mixing baking soda and vinegar?

Materials

- ¼ cup (56 grams) of baking soda
- ¼ cup (60 milliliters) of vinegar
- 1 small, empty water bottle
- 1 balloon
- 1 funnel

Procedure

1. Stretch the balloon out before using it.
2. Using the funnel, fill the balloon with the baking soda.
3. Pour the vinegar into the empty water bottle.
4. Attach the opening of the balloon to the mouth of the water bottle—be careful not to get any baking soda into the bottle.
5. Count to three and lift up the part of the balloon that contains the baking soda so that the baking soda falls into the bottle.

Questions

1. What are the physical properties of the baking soda?
2. What are the physical properties of the vinegar?
3. What happened inside the water bottle when you added the baking soda to the vinegar? What did you see in the bottle?
4. Did anything happen to the balloon? If so, what do you think caused it?
5. What type of change occurred inside the bottle when you added the baking soda to the vinegar?

Lesson Plans in Science - 14

Living and Non-living things

Living and Non-living things

Learning Objectives

Students will be able to ask and answer questions about living and nonliving things to clarify their thinking and classifications.

Introduction

Ask the class if they are living or nonliving.

Ask students if their pets at home are living or nonliving.

Ask students to identify what they need to survive. Write "food," "water," "shelter," and "air" on the board.

Explain to students that today they will be learning about living and nonliving things.

Teacher Activity

Ask students to think of a question, or something they want to know, about living and nonliving things. Remind students that questions start with who, what, when where, why or how. Allow students think time, and choose student volunteers to ask questions. Write questions on the board (e.g., How do you know if something is living? or What can living things do?"

Play students the *Living and Nonliving Things* video.

Check whether the class is able to answer any of their questions following the video. Allow students to turn and talk to a partner to answer the following comprehension questions about key details from the video:

What are some examples from the video of living things? What are some examples from the video of nonliving things? How does Cookie Monster know that rock is not alive?

Ideate

Read students the story *What's Alive.*

As you read the text, invite students to turn and talk to a partner to ask and answer questions about what they see in the illustrations. Write example questions on the board such as:

What is living in the picture? What is nonliving in the picture? Is a living or nonliving?

Ask students questions about key details from the text such as: How are you the same as a cat?

What do living things need to survive?

Then, sing the following song together to the tune of Frere Jacques:

It is living! It is living! I know why!

I know why!

It eats and breathes and grows, It eats and breathes and grows, It's alive!

It's alive!

Design

Now, place two hula hoops on the ground. Label one "living" and one "nonliving." Present the class with various living and nonliving objects such as a banana, a truck and a plant.

Have each student come to the hula hoops and place objects in the hula hoop in either the living or the nonliving category. Have students repeat chorally, "Is a____ living or nonliving?"

Model looking at an item, and asking a question to clarify whether the object is living or nonliving. Think back to the information presented in the video and ask, "Does this object grow and change?"

Continue until every student has had a chance to ask questions to clarify whether their object is living or nonliving. Allow students to take turns answering the questions, and classifying the objects.

Enrichment:

Have students in need of enrichment draw objects on a paper that are living.

Support:

Read additional books about living and nonliving things to students who are struggling with the concept.

Experiment

Observe whether students are able to correctly classify living and nonliving things in the sorting activity. Listen to assess whether students are able to ask and answer questions about key details from the read aloud and video.

Assessment

Have each student go around the room and find a nonliving object. Remind students to ask a question, "Is this living or nonliving?" Have students then answer their question using information and details from the video and text.

CHAPTER SIXTEEN

Conclusion

1. Science Encourages Creativity

Experimenting requires trial and error. Kids learn that if something doesn't work the first time, try it again. Giving them room to try new ideas fosters creativity and resourcefulness. Science is a study that starts with a question. Answers are not given right away; instead, students search them out.

2. Science Develops Analytical Thinking Skills

To analyze something means to look closer, or examine. Science does that by having students make observations. They can later predict an outcome or form a conclusion based on what they see. Students can learn problem-solving and other skills through the Scientific Method.

3. Science Improves Communication Skills

Writing:

Keeping a science notebook can develop organization in student writing. Give them a specific model—for example, have students write their own procedure for doing an experiment. This way they will learn to write in a clear and well-developed way.

Reading:

Following instructions is important when doing a dissection or chemistry experiment. Students will have to learn to read each detail of a procedure or lab manual.

Verbal Skills:

Science is also an opportunity to work with others. Your children will learn to communicate ideas in a respectful way, and set a common goal.

4. Science Develops a Love of Learning

When you discover something on your own, that thing has power. It resonates inside you, nurturing possibilities and opening doors. By seeking answers scientists learn to pursue knowledge. Becoming a self-taught or independent learner is a lifelong process. Once you have caught the love of learning it never goes away.

5. Science Broadens Our Perspective

Science changes how you see other subjects, including art and music. Someone may examine works of art with more interest after studying how our eyes see color. Students may notice the variety of tones in orchestra instruments after studying sound waves. An understanding of science can also add interest to everyday activities like taking a walk, or shoveling snow. Science explains the world around us. But through the explanation, we delight and wonder.

The Importance Of Science Education In Schools

1. Knowledge

Science education gives students the opportunity to gain a better knowledge of how and why things function. Science can teach children about the world that surrounds them. Everything from human anatomy to techniques of transportation, science can reveal the mechanisms and the reasons for complicated systems. The information gained from science can be used to grasp new ideas, make educated choices and pursue the pursuit of a new passion.

Furthermore, since science provides tangible or visual proof of many of the facts we see on the screen and in books, kids and teens are able to increase their knowledge and remember information more effectively.

2. Problem Solving Skills

Children can get an appreciation for skepticism through studying science. Science can also create curiosity that helps students understand and formulate questions on the information they have accumulated. A lot of students find science exciting and fascinating, and consequently, explore new areas of interest in science. Science gives youngsters the idea that they can help solve world problems which is a good idea. Science helps children think rationally and to solve issues.

3. Boost Critical Thinking

Concepts in science typically start with an idea and then an experiment that proves the idea using scientific techniques and analyses. The scientific method outlines a logical approach to new topics, ensuring that students are able to connect theoretical and practical work. Understanding the connection between the theories and research has advantages that are applicable to all disciplines and areas of life. Like gas to a stove, science provides the energy that accelerates young minds to peak performance.

4. Cultivates A Passion For Learning

The fascination of discovering how the sun sets to the east, why the sky is blue, how fish breathe in wat, and other amazing everyday events is naturally intriguing. Science stimulates the natural curiosity that drives learners and inspires them to discover the mysteries of the world around them. An approach that is hands-on draws the attention of many. The chance to demonstrate the concepts of science in person can inspire a love of learning.

5. Uplifts Many Disciplines

To be able to comprehend science, it is necessary to have knowledge of other subjects of study. For instance, understanding mathematical concepts is a crucial necessity that can be useful for quantitative and qualitative analysis. Scientific methodology is built on technical abilities like the careful study of what is happening around you as well as being able to carry out controlled experiments. The presentation of results in scientific reports is a way to teach the value of thoroughness and objectivity.

6. Holds The Key To Future

It's hard to imagine one aspect of life that isn't influenced by technology in some way. It's a vital component of many areas that range from agriculture to high-tech, and everything in between. The future generation needs an education in science that will aid them in their preparation for the future. Science can be useful in demonstrating to students the health and environmental consequences of pollutants like smoking tobacco, as well as the dangers of addiction to substances.

7. Technology

Science is a way to teach the basics of how specific devices work. This can help children come up with their own ideas and may even help invent new technologies in the near future. Understanding how microscopes, telescopes as well as other instruments used in labs perform can help you evaluate objects and distinguish the difference. This fundamental knowledge of technology can also assist in the resolution of minor issues in electronic objects in your home.

CHAPTER SEVENTEEN

References

- https://www.theasianschool.net/blog/importance-of-science-education-in-schools/
- https://epublications.regis.edu/cgi/viewcontent.cgi?article=1096&context=theses
- https://learning-center.homesciencetools.com/article/why-science/
- https://creativeeducator.tech4learning.com/science
- https://www.education.com/lesson-plans/science/

Disclaimer

The information provided in this book is for educational
purposes only. It is the view presented by the author with
references to various classroom experiences and references
from e-resources.